COLLEGE SPORTS TODAY

COLLEGE SPORTS TODAY

IRISH LEGENDS!

THE NOTRE DAME FIGHTING IRISH STORY

GWEN GRIFFIN

CREATIVE EDUCATION

Published by Creative Education
123 South Broad Street, Mankato, Minnesota 56001
Creative Education is an imprint of The Creative Company

Designed by Stephanie Blumenthal
Production design by The Design Lab
Editorial assistance by John Nichols

Photos by: Allsport USA, AP/Wide World Photos, Cheryl A. Ertelt,
SportsChrome, and UPI/Corbis-Bettmann

Library of Congress Cataloging-in-Publication Data

Griffin, Gwen, 1957–
Irish Legends! the Notre Dame Fighting Irish story / by Gwen Griffin.
p. cm. — (College football today)
Summary: Examines the history of the University of Notre Dame football program.
ISBN: 0-88682-982-8

1. University of Notre Dame—Football—History—Juvenile literature. 2. Notre Dame Fighting Irish
(Football team)—History—Juvenile literature. [1. Notre Dame Fighting Irish (Football team)—History.
2. Football—History.] I. Title. II. Series: College football today (Mankato, Minn.)

GV958.U6G75   1999
796.332'63'0977289—dc21   98-30937

First Edition

2 4 6 8 9 7 5 3 1

A walk around the picturesque Notre Dame campus on a brisk November day is like a stroll through college football history. Among the long roll call of Fighting Irish greats are such legends as George Gipp, Joe Montana, Alan Page, and Tim Brown. Under the guidance of some of football's most legendary coaches, these stars and many more have built the highest winning percentage (nearly 76 percent) in Division I football history and have made Notre Dame one of the most revered and prestigious college football homes in America. Football at Notre Dame is more than just a game for students, alumni, and fans—it's an experience. It's the Victory March, the leprechaun, the Friday night pep rallies, the gold helmets, the blue jerseys, and the unconquerable spirit of the Irish athletes.

1987 HEISMAN TROPHY

WINNER AND ALL-AMERICAN

TIM BROWN.

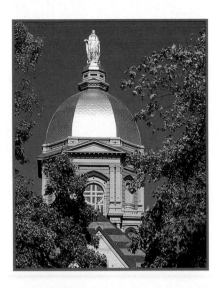

THE NOTRE DAME

STEEPLE IN SOUTH BEND

(ABOVE); THE FAMOUS

GOLD HELMETS (BELOW)

CHEER, CHEER FOR OLD NOTRE DAME

In 1842, Father Edward Sorin, a young French priest, set up a college with $310 in cash and three old log buildings in the middle of the northern Indiana frontier. The college sat near a curve in the St. Joseph River that came to be known as "South Bend." Sorin named the school "L'Universite de Notre Dame du Lac"—the University of Our Lady of the Lake. Programs included not only college subjects, but also elementary and preparatory classes, as well as a manual labor school.

Before the Civil War, the most popular sport in America was not football or baseball, but prize fighting. Many of the most famous fighters were Irish immigrants, who were known for their rowdiness and willingness to fight. These feisty Irish-Americans are probably the origin of the nickname "Fighting Irish." Although the moniker actually began as an insult, Notre Dame athletes—who called themselves the "Catholics" in the 1800s—were proud of their scrappy image and adopted the new name in 1927.

Baseball was the most popular sport at Notre Dame until well after the Civil War. The school played its first football game on November 23, 1887, against Michigan, losing to the Wolverines 8–0. The sport took a while to catch on in South Bend; in fact, the team didn't even have a coach until 1894. The school

TONY RICE GUIDED THE IRISH FROM 1987 TO 1989.

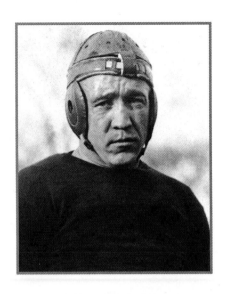

newspaper reported on one home game in 1899: "There was small interest aroused in last Saturday's contest with Lake Forest. . . . Those that went to see it were there mostly out of curiosity." Notre Dame won 38–0.

Notre Dame's strong athletic tradition has been part of the school's foundation since the beginning. Since the school sat out in the country, surrounded by forests and farm fields, students were miles from the nearest big-city attractions. Notre Dame did not permit social fraternities, and women were not allowed into the school until 1972. For entertainment, residence halls each had their own sports teams and cheers. The rallies that helped a hall intimidate its opponents evolved into the famed Friday night pep rallies of today. From this enthusiasm also came "The Notre Dame Victory March," the school's anthem and one of the best-known songs in America.

ROCKNE RAISES THE BAR

In the early days, football at Notre Dame was run by team captains, student managers, and part-time coaches. The first full-time coach and athletic director, Jesse Harper, was hired in 1913, just before the outbreak of World War I. Under Harper's guidance, Notre Dame soon gained a national reputation for its football prowess.

Before Harper's first season, Notre Dame's bid to join the Western Conference had been rejected, causing scheduling problems for the new coach. With his team

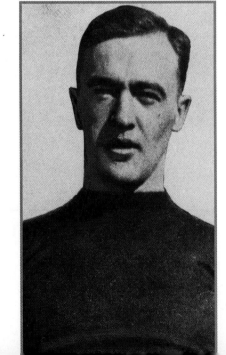

forced to play as an independent, Coach Harper knew that he would have to take his squad east to earn some respect. One eastern team Harper targeted was Army, which ruled college football at the time and was expected to give Notre Dame a thorough pasting.

After an all-day train ride, 18 Notre Dame players stepped onto the field to face the Cadets on November 1, 1913. Things did not go well at first for the Irish. They fumbled on their first possession, and Army recovered the ball deep in Notre Dame territory. The Irish took a steady pounding from the powerful Army line, but the gritty Notre Dame defenders held strong, forcing the Cadets to give up the ball.

Then, an amazing development unfolded. Notre Dame quarterback Gus Dorais began to shred the rugged Army defense through the air, firing spirals to senior end Knute Rockne. Although the forward pass was generally considered an offensive gimmick in that era, Dorais connected on 14 of 17 passes for 243 total yards in the air—unheard-of numbers in 1913.

With its deadly passing and several long running gains from Ray Eichenlaub, Notre Dame rocked Army 35–13. A young cadet named Dwight Eisenhower watched from the bench in disbelief. Notre Dame's victory thrust it into the national spotlight, and teams from all over the East lined up to play against the Irish. Coach Harper's scheduling problems were over.

JIM CROWLEY (ABOVE), A MEMBER OF THE FAMED FOUR HORSEMEN (BELOW)

THIS MURAL ON THE HESBURGH MEMORIAL LIBRARY HAS BEEN NICKNAMED "TOUCHDOWN JESUS."

Knute Rockne, one half of Notre Dame's lethal passing attack, was a young Norwegian immigrant who first played football in the sandlots of Chicago. After graduating from high school, he worked at a Chicago post office to save enough money to go to Notre Dame. Once there, he lettered in track, played football, wrote for the student newspaper, played in the school orchestra, took a major role in every school play, and even made the finals of the school's marble tournament. Rockne was also an outstanding student who graduated with an "A" average.

When Rockne was offered a job as a graduate assistant in the chemistry department at Notre Dame, he told school officials he would take the job only if he could help Jesse Harper coach the football team. When Harper retired in 1917, Rockne was named as his successor. During his 13 years as head coach, Rockne and his teams captured six national championships and the attention of the nation.

Because of their frequent and long road trips, Rockne's team earned various nicknames, including the "Ramblers," "Rockne's Rovers," and the "Wandering Irish." Whatever they were called, the Notre Dame teams' accomplishments spoke for themselves: a 1925 Rose Bowl victory, five unbeaten and untied seasons, and 20 first-team All-Americans. Rockne's 105–12–5 career record represented a winning percentage of .881—the highest in either college or professional football.

Rockne, who was inducted into the National Football Foundation Hall of Fame in 1951, didn't just win games—he revolutionized the

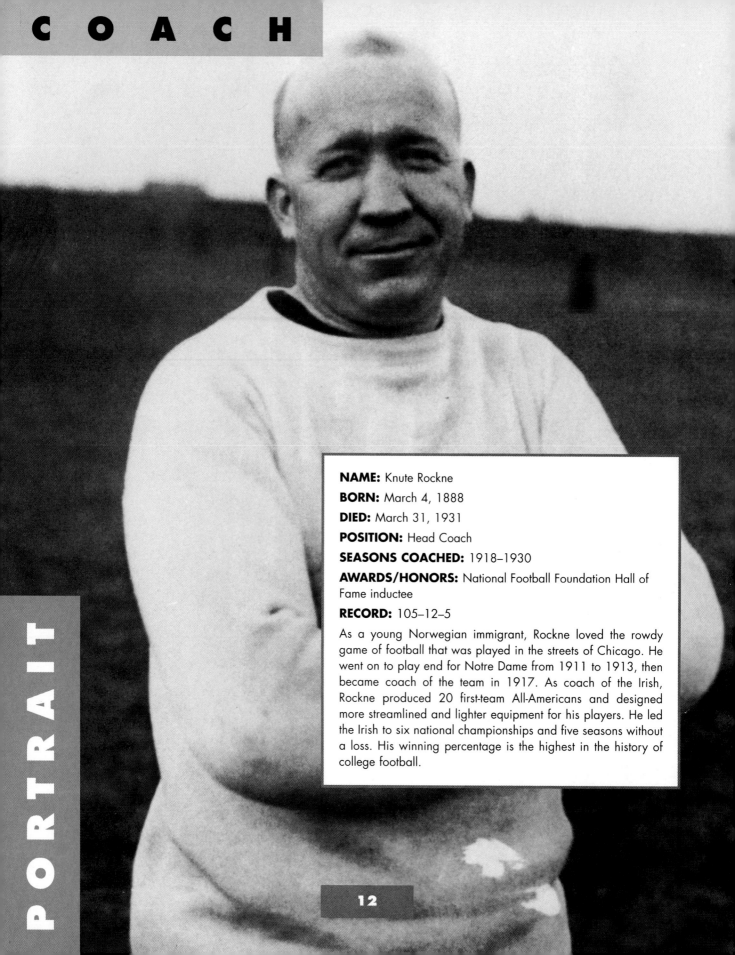

NAME: Knute Rockne

BORN: March 4, 1888

DIED: March 31, 1931

POSITION: Head Coach

SEASONS COACHED: 1918–1930

AWARDS/HONORS: National Football Foundation Hall of Fame inductee

RECORD: 105–12–5

As a young Norwegian immigrant, Rockne loved the rowdy game of football that was played in the streets of Chicago. He went on to play end for Notre Dame from 1911 to 1913, then became coach of the team in 1917. As coach of the Irish, Rockne produced 20 first-team All-Americans and designed more streamlined and lighter equipment for his players. He led the Irish to six national championships and five seasons without a loss. His winning percentage is the highest in the history of college football.

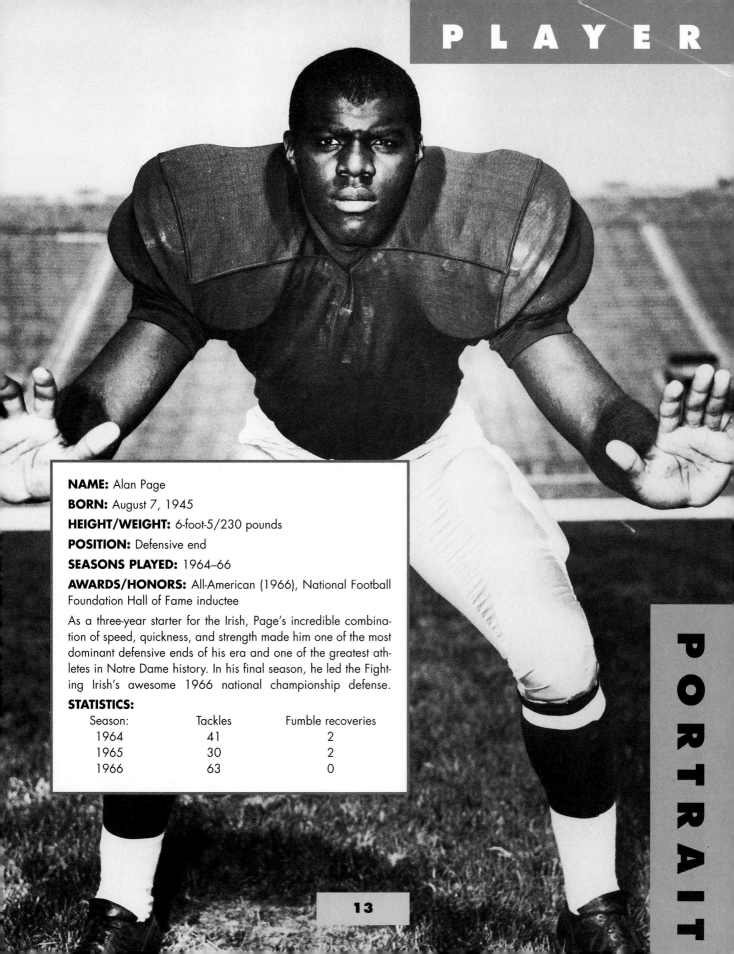

NAME: Alan Page

BORN: August 7, 1945

HEIGHT/WEIGHT: 6-foot-5/230 pounds

POSITION: Defensive end

SEASONS PLAYED: 1964–66

AWARDS/HONORS: All-American (1966), National Football Foundation Hall of Fame inductee

As a three-year starter for the Irish, Page's incredible combination of speed, quickness, and strength made him one of the most dominant defensive ends of his era and one of the greatest athletes in Notre Dame history. In his final season, he led the Fighting Irish's awesome 1966 national championship defense.

STATISTICS:

Season:	Tackles	Fumble recoveries
1964	41	2
1965	30	2
1966	63	0

PORTRAIT

13

sport. He designed his own equipment and uniforms to reduce bulk and weight and to increase protection. He was the master of pregame psychology and always downplayed his team's talent in an effort to outsmart opposing coaches. He believed that passing was half of football strategy in an era when most coaches kept the ball on the ground. He helped design Notre Dame Stadium. He even played a coach in a Broadway production called "Good News" and was offered the part in Hollywood's film version. It was a role he would never get to play.

On March 31, 1931, Rockne took Transcontinental-Western flight 599 from Kansas City to Los Angeles to meet with movie producers. Shortly after takeoff, the plane iced up and crashed in a wheat field in Kansas. There were no survivors.

"THE ROCKET" RAGHIB

ISMAIL (ABOVE);

RONALD REAGAN AT

NOTRE DAME (BELOW)

TO WIN ONE FOR THE "GIPPER"

Of all the legends in Notre Dame football history, perhaps the most widely known is that of George Gipp and Knute Rockne. When Rockne first saw Gipp drop-kicking footballs 60 to 70 yards just for fun, the coach was convinced that he needed Gipp for the team. But Gipp had come to Notre Dame to play baseball and had never played football before. Rockne persuaded Gipp to

FLANKER LAKE DAWSON

use his talents on the football field, where he proved to be a versatile player who could run, pass, and punt. Gipp led Notre Dame in rushing and passing during his last three seasons (1918, 1919, and 1920). After football season was over, Gipp played center field for Notre Dame's baseball team and had dreams of playing for the Chicago Cubs after graduation.

In 1920, Gipp was named the Outstanding College Player in America, but an injury kept him out of the last game against Northwestern. However, when the crowd began to chant, "We want Gipp!" in the fourth quarter, the coach sent him into the game. Soon after that final game, Gipp got strep throat. The infection turned into pneumonia, and on December 14, George Gipp died at the age of 25.

Eight years later, an injury-riddled Notre Dame team was set to face an undefeated Army squad. After reading a newspaper story on the late George Gipp, Rockne used Gipp's legend to inspire his ailing team. In a now-famous pregame speech, Rockne said to his team, "The day before he died, George Gipp asked me to wait until the situation seemed hopeless—then ask a Notre Dame team to go out and beat Army for him. This is the day, and you are the team." The Irish defeated Army 12–6 that day.

This legend was immortalized in the movie "Knute Rockne—All American." George Gipp, portrayed by actor Ronald Reagan, was on his deathbed as he said to his coach, "I've got to go,

Rock. It's all right. I'm not afraid. Some time, Rock, when the team is up against it, when things are wrong and the breaks are beating the boys—tell them to go in there with all they've got and win just one for the Gipper. I don't know where I'll be then, Rock. But I'll know about it, and I'll be happy."

Now, more than 70 years later, whenever a player or team faces seemingly unbeatable odds, the old phrase "Win one for the Gipper" inspires them to dig down and give it their all just one more time.

THE IRISH RIDE TO A LEGEND

A perfect 10–0 record marked the 1924 Notre Dame team's efforts and gave the school its first national championship. But it was a sportswriter who helped bring lasting fame to South Bend as he reported on the Notre Dame-Army game played on October 18, 1924, at the Polo Grounds in New York.

HORSEMEN MILLER,

LAYDEN, AND CROWLEY

(ABOVE, LEFT TO RIGHT);

TACKLE FRANK LEAHY

(BELOW)

New York Herald Tribune writer Grantland Rice described the game: "Outlined against a blue-gray October sky, the Four Horsemen ride again. In dramatic lore they are known as famine, pestilence, destruction, and death. These are only aliases. Their real names are [Harry] Stuhldreher, [Don] Miller, [Jim] Crowley, and [Elmer] Layden. They formed the crest of the South Bend cyclone before which another fighting Army team was swept over the precipice at the Polo Grounds this afternoon. . . ." This account changed the style of sports reporting and propelled Notre Dame's backfield into legendary status.

After a 13–7 win over Army, the team returned to South Bend, and George Strickler, the Notre Dame student press assistant, rounded up four workhorses for a photo shoot. Strickler sent a picture of the players on horseback to the wire services, and newspapers all over the country reproduced the photo along with Rice's account of the game. "At the time, I didn't realize the impact it would have," Crowley later said. "After the splurge in the press, the sports fans of the nation got interested in us along with other sportswriters."

In the weeks that followed the win over Army, the wire services continued to distribute the photo and story of "The Four Horsemen." In the 1920s, before television was invented, most fans could never see their sports heroes in action; they could only read about them in newspapers. The press took advantage of the hype created by "The Four Horsemen" and used the publicity for all it

was worth. Strickler sold hundreds of prints to newspapers, magazines, and fans around the country. The marketing of college football had begun.

All four of the "Horsemen" went on to coach college teams and eventually rode their way into the National Football Foundation Hall of Fame and into Notre Dame history.

RALLY SONS OF NOTRE DAME

With Knute Rockne's untimely and tragic death, the responsibilities of coaching "America's Team" went to Heartley "Hunk" Anderson, who had been an All-American guard at Notre Dame. Anderson coached the Irish for three seasons, compiling a 16–9–2 record. When he left South Bend, another Notre Dame legend stepped in. Best remembered as an All-American fullback and one of the Four Horsemen of 1924, Elmer Layden coached his alma mater for seven years in the shadow of his former coach and mentor. It was a tough job living up to the standards of "Rockne's System," but Layden pulled off seven winning seasons and finished his coaching career at Notre Dame at 47–13–3.

Rockne's influence continued when Frank Leahy was hired as head coach in 1941. A tackle on Rockne's last three teams, Leahy had graduated from Notre Dame in 1931 and coached at Georgetown, Michigan State, and Boston College. Except for a two-year stint in the Navy during World War II, Leahy coached the Irish from 1941 through 1953.

In 1943, Leahy and Notre Dame—which had only two returning starters from the previous year—faced a season with seven opponents ranked among the top 13 by the Associated Press.

HARRY STUHLDREHER

ORCHESTRATED THE

OFFENSE IN 1924.

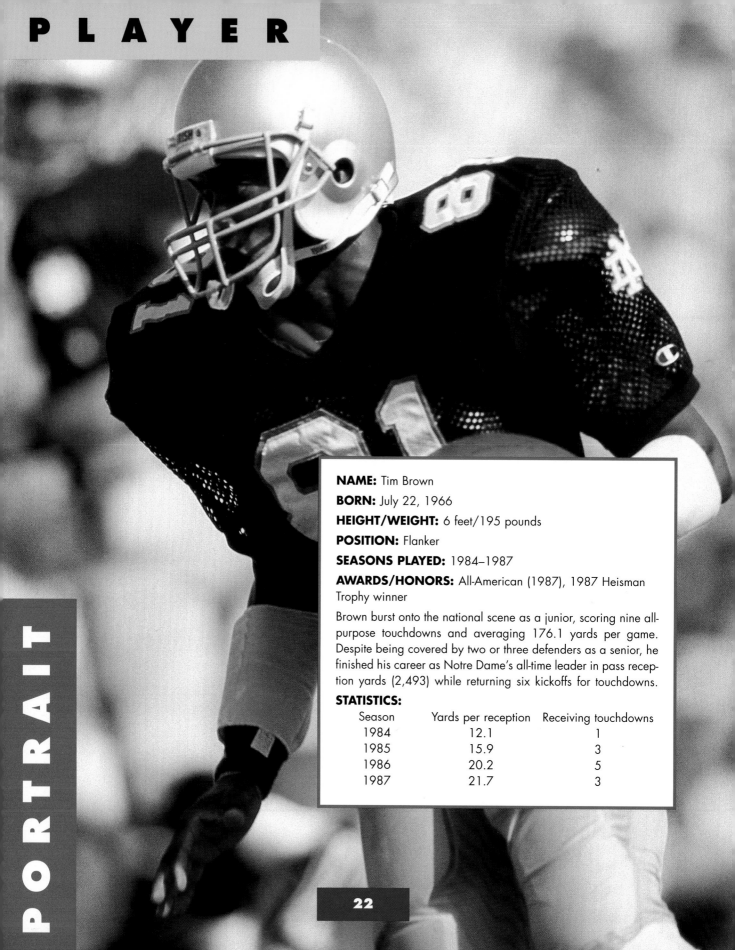

NAME: Tim Brown

BORN: July 22, 1966

HEIGHT/WEIGHT: 6 feet/195 pounds

POSITION: Flanker

SEASONS PLAYED: 1984–1987

AWARDS/HONORS: All-American (1987), 1987 Heisman Trophy winner

Brown burst onto the national scene as a junior, scoring nine all-purpose touchdowns and averaging 176.1 yards per game. Despite being covered by two or three defenders as a senior, he finished his career as Notre Dame's all-time leader in pass reception yards (2,493) while returning six kickoffs for touchdowns.

STATISTICS:

Season	Yards per reception	Receiving touchdowns
1984	12.1	1
1985	15.9	3
1986	20.2	5
1987	21.7	3

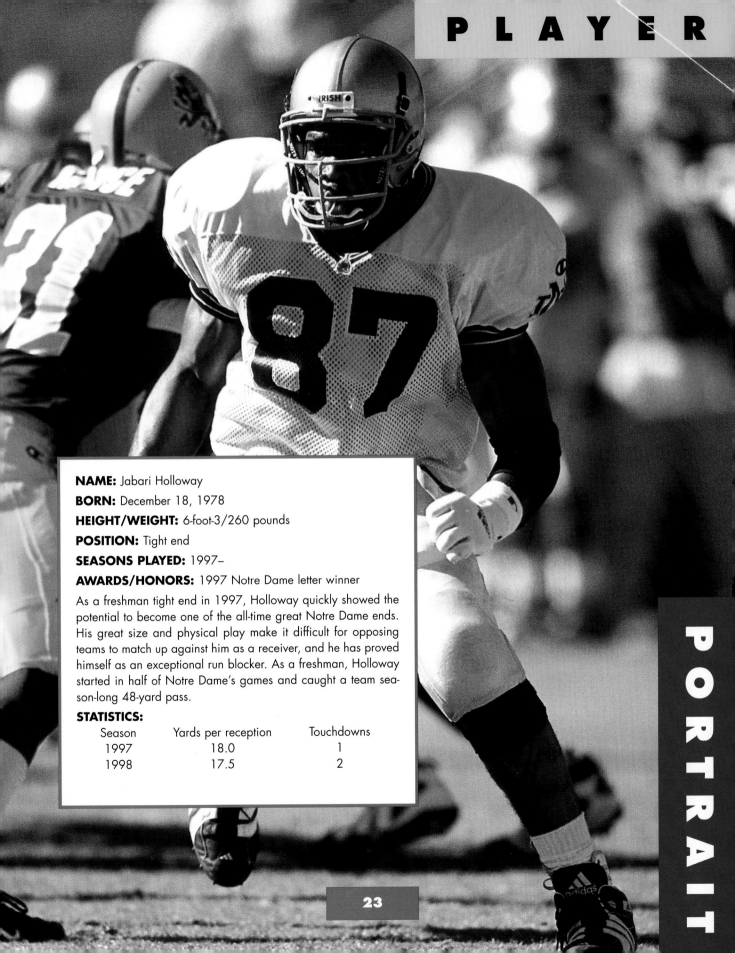

NAME: Jabari Holloway

BORN: December 18, 1978

HEIGHT/WEIGHT: 6-foot-3/260 pounds

POSITION: Tight end

SEASONS PLAYED: 1997–

AWARDS/HONORS: 1997 Notre Dame letter winner

As a freshman tight end in 1997, Holloway quickly showed the potential to become one of the all-time great Notre Dame ends. His great size and physical play make it difficult for opposing teams to match up against him as a receiver, and he has proved himself as an exceptional run blocker. As a freshman, Holloway started in half of Notre Dame's games and caught a team season-long 48-yard pass.

STATISTICS:

Season	Yards per reception	Touchdowns
1997	18.0	1
1998	17.5	2

PORTRAIT

Guiding a new T-formation offense, quarterback Angelo Bertelli and halfback Creighton Miller helped Notre Dame outscore its opponents 261–31 on its way to a convincing 6–0 start. In the midst of World War II, Bertelli was called into service in the Marine Corps, leaving John Lujack to take over. Lujack kept the team rolling, and the Irish were named national champions that year. Bertelli's performance earned him a place in history as Notre Dame's first Heisman Trophy winner.

Leahy won five national championships, led the Irish to four undefeated seasons, and compiled an 87–11–9 record. He coached such Irish greats as 1949 Heisman Trophy winner Leon Hart and All-American tackles Bill Fischer and George Conner.

But despite Leahy's success, a coaching decision during his final year left a smirch on Notre Dame's reputation. In a close game against Iowa on November 21, 1953, Leahy needed extra timeouts and instructed one of his players to fake an injury to stop the clock. The player did as he was told, and Notre Dame managed to score and avoid the loss. The press called Leahy's team the "Fainting Irish," and angry fans condemned the tactic as a setback to the Notre Dame tradition.

THE ERA OF ARA

Leahy retired in 1954 and was replaced by Notre Dame graduate Terry Brennan (1954–58), then Joe Kuharich (1959–62). In 1964, Ara Parseghian was hired as head coach, becoming the first Fighting Irish coach since Jesse Harper who had not gone to school at Notre Dame. Parseghian was young, ambitious, and well-organized. In 11 years at Notre Dame, he won three national championships, the 1970 Cotton Bowl, the 1973 Sugar Bowl, and the 1975 Orange Bowl.

The Sugar Bowl matchup between Notre Dame and Alabama in 1973 was a classic confrontation between two undefeated, highly ranked teams with long traditions. Notre Dame was led by ace quarterback Tom Clements, burly tight end Dave Casper, and ball-hawking defensive back Mike Townsend. Alabama featured legendary coach Bear Bryant's trademark power running game and swarming defense.

The Irish opened the game with an incredible defensive effort that kept the Crimson Tide from gaining a single

IRISH HALFBACK BILL WOLSKI (ABOVE, #35); COACH ARA PARSEGHIAN (BELOW)

yard in the first quarter, and Notre Dame jumped out to a 6–0 lead. But the Tide fought back, and by the end of the third quarter, the score stood at 21–17, Irish in front.

The fourth quarter turned wild as the teams committed a combined three turnovers in the span of 90 seconds. Alabama capitalized on the miscues with a touchdown that put it ahead 23–21. Working against the clock and a fierce 'Bama defense, the Irish came roaring back. A series of hard runs, followed by a 30-yard pass from Clements to Casper, took the Irish to the Crimson Tide 15-yard line. With 4:26 left in the game, Notre Dame kicker Bob Thomas booted a 25-yard field goal for the win, sealing the Irish's perfect 11–0 season. "This was not only a great game for Notre Dame," Parseghian said, "it was a great game for college football." Despite his team's loss, Alabama's Bryant had to agree: "It was the kind of game you could sink your teeth into."

The Irish would win another national championship in 1977 with Coach Dan Devine at the helm. Notre Dame defeated top-ranked and unbeaten Texas 38–10, with the "Comeback Kid," Joe Montana, leading the Irish to the overwhelming 28-point victory. Montana threw for 1,604 yards and 11 touchdowns that year, and in 1978, he became only the third Fighting Irish quarterback

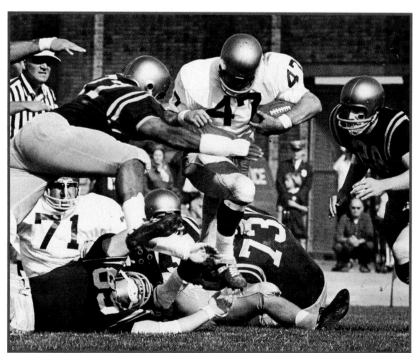

to throw for more than 2,000 yards in a single season. He ended his career at Notre Dame with 4,121 passing yards and went on to become one of the National Football League's all-time greats.

REBUILDING THE FIRE

From 1981 to 1985, the Fighting Irish made only two bowl appearances under head coach Gerry Faust. Although Faust compiled a 30–26–1 record with three winning seasons, his teams did not produce the kind of dominating performances that fans and alumni had come to expect from Notre Dame teams. He resigned in 1985.

Lou Holtz took over the Fighting Irish program in 1986, and in 11 seasons, he guided his teams to a record of 100–30–2. A 1988 national championship—earned via a 34–21 victory over an unbeaten West Virginia team in the Fiesta Bowl—capped off a perfect 12–0 season. Like Leahy, Parseghian, and Devine, Holtz had led Notre Dame to a national crown in just his third season as head coach.

Early in the 1996 season, Holtz surpassed Rockne's record of 122 games as head coach of the Irish. At the end of that

ACADEMIC HALL OF FAME QUARTERBACK JOE THEISMAN (ABOVE); COACH GERRY FAUST (BELOW)

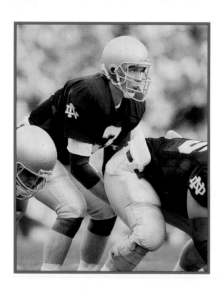

season, Holtz stepped down to pursue a career in broadcasting before becoming the South Carolina Gamecocks head coach in 1998. His 100 wins at Notre Dame are second only to the 105 victories of Rockne. During his term, Holtz mentored Fighting Irish greats such as Heisman Trophy-winning wide receiver Tim Brown, standout quarterback Tony Rice, defensive demon Chris Zorich, and star running backs Ricky Watters and Jerome Bettis.

Coach Bob Davie, who accepted the daunting task of carrying on the Irish tradition in 1997, knew that maintaining the level of excellence set by previous Notre Dame coaches would not be easy. "When you look at those names . . . and what they've achieved," Davie said, "it can be a little overwhelming." Although Davie's squad dropped four straight games early in the 1997 season, Notre Dame rebounded to finish at 7–6.

Over the years, Notre Dame has earned high respect not only on the football field, but also in the classroom. The school has an overall graduation rate of 98 percent among its football players who remain for four years. The university has won the College Football Association's Academic Achievement award five times in 17 years, and Irish greats Joe Theisman, Dave Casper, and Bob Thomas have all been enshrined in the GTE Academic All-America Hall of Fame.

RON POWLUS

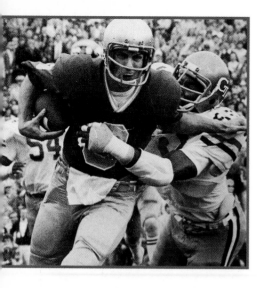

THE TRADITION CONTINUES

In 1998, Notre Dame roared back into the national spotlight, posting a 9–2 regular-season mark. Led by the school's all-time leading rusher, halfback Autry Denson, the resurgent Irish earned a berth in the Gator Bowl versus Georgia Tech. Unfortunately, the Irish lost the game 35–28 despite 130 yards and three touchdowns from Denson. "In my four years, we've been through a lot," said the hard-charging Denson. "We had some tough times, but I think Coach Davie has the program heading back to the top again."

Looking forward, Davie will rely on defensive stalwarts such as linebacker Grant Irons and cornerback Deke Cooper to put the clamps on opposing teams, while game-breaking receivers Joey Getherall and Raki Nelson will be counted on to stretch defenses with their blazing speed. Highly recruited running back Tony Fisher appears to be a rising star, and hulking tight end Jabari Holloway poses a constant threat as both a receiver and blocker.

With a strong tradition in both academics and athletics, Notre Dame is a school that seems to have it all, including a new stadium, a new coach, and a football tradition as strong as the invincible spirit of the Irish. As former Fighting Irish quarterback Joe Theisman once said, "If you could find a way to bottle the Notre Dame spirit, you could light up the universe."

THE "COMEBACK KID,"

JOE MONTANA (ABOVE);

LINEBACKER GRANT

IRONS (BELOW)